Drama Workshops for Young Children

10 Drama Workshops for Young Children Based on Children's Stories

by
Julie Meighan

First published in 2020
by
JemBooks
Cork,
Ireland
dramastartbooks.com

ISBN: 978-1-9163195-3-0

All rights reserved.

No part of this book may be reproduced or utilised in any form or by any electronic, digital or mechanical means, including information storage, photocopying, filming, recording, video recording and retrieval systems, without prior permission in writing from the publisher. The only exception is by a reviewer, who may quote short excerpts in a review. The moral rights of the author have been asserted.

Text Copyright © 2020, Julie Meighan

Contents

Introduction..1
Drama Strategies Glossary..3
Drama Workshops...13
The Enormous Turnip..15
The Hare and the Tortoise...20
The Lion and the Clever Rabbit...................................24
Goldilocks and the Three Bears...................................29
The Lion and the Mouse..36
The Three Little Pigs...40
The Little Red Hen...47
Chicken Licken..53
The Ants and the Grasshopper....................................60
The Three Billy Goats Gruff...65

Introduction

This book contains 10 drama workshops for young children. These fun-to-use and easy-to-follow workshops are designed for children between the ages of 3 and 7. The workshops are based on children's stories. Each story is introduced at the beginning of each workshop through a movement story or a play. The definition and aim of each drama strategy used is outlined in the drama strategy glossary at the beginning of the book. The aims of these drama workshops are to

Promote children's self-regulation
Develop children's language and communication skills
Teach children conflict resolution
Relieve children's emotional tension
Allow children to develop a sense of ownership
Promote children's social interaction skills
Empower children

Things for teachers to remember.

Always be enthusiastic. The children will be drawn to your energy and will get excited about the prospect of participating in the activity. Get involved in the drama. You may be required to help move the drama on. Reflect on the workshop. Think about what worked and didn't work and the reasons why. Never force a child to participate. Let the non-participating child observed as long as they want. Be very clear with your instructions. Ask for feedback from the children to make sure they understand what is involved and what each child must do

Drama Strategies Glossary

Name of drama strategy: Action narration.

Definition of drama strategy: A scene is performed with participants using narration to describe their actions around individual spoken lines of dialogue.

Aim of drama strategy: To describe in words the action portrayed in a scene or a mime.

Name of drama strategy: Choral speaking.

Definition of drama strategy: The children speak at the same time, the same words, with one voice.

Aim of drama strategy: (1) To promote group awareness. (2) To develop aural and listening skills.

Name of drama strategy: Collective picture drawing.

Definition of drama strategy: A drawing that is developed collectively by a group.

Aim of drama strategy: (1) To share ownership of the picture. (2) To promote teamwork, observation and active listening skills.

Name of drama strategy: Conscience alley.

Definition of drama strategy: Structured like a gauntlet, but the group plays the character's thoughts, and voices are lower in volume. A word or phrase is spoken as the character passes by individuals in the group. On one side you have the good side of the conscience, and on the other side it is the evil part of the conscience.

Aim of drama strategy: (1) To understand a character's motivations. (2) To give each child input into a character's actions. (3) To promote persuasive speech.

Name of drama strategy: Freeze frame.

Definition of drama strategy: When the action in a scene is stopped and that particular moment becomes a still image. The still image can be discussed by the participants involved or by the rest of the class.

Aim of drama strategy: To allow time for reflection or discussion of a significant moment in the scene.

Name of drama strategy: Hot-seating.

Definition of drama strategy: Participants are interviewed in character. Other members of the group asks questions that will explore the character who is sitting in the hot seat.

Aim of drama strategy: To discover a character's background and perspective.

Name of drama strategy: Improvisation.

Definition of drama strategy: Improvisation is the spontaneous invention and development of a drama without the use of a script or preparation.

Aim of drama strategy: To develop spontaneity and quick thinking in a role.

Name of drama strategy: Mime.

Definition of drama strategy: Action and storytelling without words. May be done in normal speed, slow motion, fast, and with one or more people.

Aim of drama strategy: To promote non-verbal communication.

Name of drama strategy: Occupational mime.

Definition of drama strategy: Lift a bucket, box, brush. Place the same objects on a shelf or table, place them, carefully on top of each other. Use scissors, shears, pickaxes, fishing rod. Use activities such as sewing buttons, cooking, putting on clothes, painting, cleaning windows.

Aim of drama strategy: To promote development of a role.

Name of drama strategy: Character mime.

Definition of drama strategy: Portray distinct types of characters, the young girl, the old woman, the rich lady, beggar, clown. Get children to watch people around them.

Aim of drama strategy: To use facial expression and body language to express different type of characters.

Name of drama strategy: Emotional mime.

Definition of drama strategy: These mimes are the hardest to portray. Feel, understand, convey happiness at receiving a gift. Sadness at hearing unwelcome news, shock, horror, love etc...,

Aim of drama strategy: To use facial expression and body language to portray different feelings and emotions.

Name of drama strategy: Movement.

Definition of drama strategy: Use of body as a means of communication.

Aim of drama strategy: (1) To develop self awareness, learn different ways of communication. (2) To promote balance, coordination and strength.

Name of drama strategy: Movement songs.

Definition of drama strategy: Songs that are sung accompanied by actions.

Aim of drama strategy: (1) To strengthen memory and recall. (2) To enhance hand eye coordination.

Name of drama strategy: Movement stories.

Definition of drama strategy: Stories that are read accompanied by movements, actions, sounds and/or words.

Aim of drama strategy: (1) To support active listening skills. (2) To develop fine and gross motor skills

Name of drama strategy: Role on the wall.

Definition of drama strategy: The students visually map the emotions and actions of a character on to the outline of a human figure. The students are invited to draw pictures or write words or phrases that relate to that specific character.

Aim of drama strategy: To allow the group to explore and understand a character's situation and motivation more.

Name of drama strategy: Role play.

Definition of drama strategy: Role playing allows a participant to play a character in a real or imaginary situation.

Aim of drama strategy: (1) To promote empathy and to allow the children t feel what it is liked to be someone else. (2) To create a safe distance for children to act if they are someone else.

Name of drama strategy: Slow motion.
Definition of drama strategy: It means slowing the action down. This is a theatrical device that is helpful in terms of demanding individual and group co-operation, concentration and physical self control.
Aim of drama strategy: (1) To develop movement.
(2) To give the audience a longer time to focus on a particular moment.

Name of drama strategy: Sound collage.
Definition of drama strategy: Sound, song, words, and phrases, either pre-recorded or performed live, are used to create the mood and atmosphere of a character's lived experience. The group are encouraged to think of the soundscape as having a musical shape to it and to weave the various words, statements and sounds together, orchestrating them as precisely as possible. Children can use their voices, bodies, musical instruments or any object in the room to create the soundscape. The teacher may be the conductor or a participant.
Aim of drama strategy: (1) To explore making sounds.
(2) To focus on aural skills and how it is relevant to drama.
(3) To explore vocal variety and rhythm both individually and as part of a group.

Name of drama strategy: Still image/Tableau.
Definition of drama strategy: Frozen action, a picture, book illustration, frozen time image.
Aim of drama strategy: Ownership of a shared image.

Name of drama strategy: Percieive and reflect.

Definition of drama strategy: Group discussion and share about what was seen, what was learned and what was liked.

Aim of drama strategy: (1) To allow children to express their thoughts and ideas freely and equally. (2) To encourage reasoning and reflection.

Name of drama strategy: Teacher in role.

Definition of drama strategy: Teacher takes on a role as part of the story for participants to interact with them inside the drama.

Aim of drama strategy: (1) To stimulate the imagination. (2) To help reach a consesensus. (3) To make suggestions. (4) To offer advice.

Name of drama strategy: Thought tracking.

Definition of drama strategy: Usually used in conjunction with still image work where the teacher steps into the image to ask the characters their innermost thoughts and feelings.

Aim of drama strategy: (1) To focus on the character inner thoughts. (2) To gain a better understanding of the character during a moment in time.

Name of drama strategy: Voice production.

Definition of drama strategy: The process of training and improving vocal ability.

Aim of drama strategy: To improve vocal clarity and vocal expression.

Name of drama strategy: Storytelling.

Definition of drama strategy: The story is presented through action, dialogue, and narration through an external narrator or by characters within the story.

Aim of drama strategy: To make storytelling participatory. To ensure everyone contributes.

Name of drama strategy: Sculpting/ Group sculpture.

Definition of drama strategy: An individual or members of the group model volunteers into a shape using as many members of the group and/or objects necessary, to represent a word, an idea, a situation or character.

Aim of drama strategy: (1) To stimulate imagination. (2) To promote group cohesion. (3) To create and explore 3D images.

Name of drama strategy: Talking objects.

Definition of drama strategy: Talking objects are objects in a drama that can talk. The objects might be within any setting and can belong to any character, e.g., children can enter one at a time and place themselves as objects in the space. The children become the objects (as in physical theatre) and once in place, they are able to tell a little about themselves, the person they belong to and maybe open to answering questions, e.g., about the comings and goings in the room. Another way of presenting talking objects is to hold a real object, e.g., a photograph. Whoever holds the object is empowered to talk as if they are the object. The object can be passed around so that several people have the opportunity to talk as the object.

Aim of drama strategy: (1) To encourage and require active listening and co-operation. (2) To actively support their understanding of personification.

Drama Workshops

The Enormous Turnip

Each child finds a space and sits down. Each child or a group of children are assigned a specific word and a corresponding action. The narrator/teacher reads the story aloud, and when the children hear their word, they must jump up and do their actions. The words are in bold to assist the teacher.

Word: Action/sound.
Old Man: Hunch and walk with a walking stick.
Turnip: Curl up body and make as small as possible.
Pull/ Pulled: Mime pulling a rope.
Wife: Mime stirring a pot.
Boy: Mime playing football.
Girl: Mime skipping.
Dog: Move like a dog and bark.
Cat: Move like a cat and meow.
Mouse: Move like a mouse and squeak.
Soup: Everyone drinks the soup from a bowl.

Once upon a time, there lived a little old **man**. One day, he planted a **turnip** seed in his garden. "This **turnip** is going to be very big and very sweet," said the old **man**. The **turnip** grew and grew, and the old **man** decided it was time to dig up the **turnip**. He **pulled** and **pulled,** but he couldn't **pull** up

the **turnip**. He said, "I know, I will ask my **wife** to help me. **Wife**! **Wife**! Please help me to **pull** up the **turnip**." His wife came and helped him. They **pulled** and **pulled,** but they couldn't **pull** up the **turnip**. The **wife** said, "I know, I will ask the **boy** to help us. **Boy**! **Boy**! Please help us to **pull** up the **turnip**." The **boy** came and helped them.
They **pulled** and **pulled** but they couldn't **pull** up the **turnip**. The **boy** said, "I know; I will ask the **girl** to help us. **Girl**! **Girl**! Please help us to **pull** up the **turnip**." The **girl** came and helped them. They **pulled** and **pulled,** but they couldn't **pull** up the **turnip**. The **girl** said, "I know, I will ask the **dog** to help us. **Dog**! **Dog**! Please help us to **pull** up the **turnip**."
The **dog** came and helped them. They **pulled** and **pulled,** but they couldn't **pull** up the **turnip**. The dog said, "I will ask the **cat** to help us. **Cat**! **Cat**! Please help us to pull up the **turnip**." The **cat** came and helped them.
They **pulled** and **pulled,** but they couldn't **pull** up the **turnip**. The **cat** said, "I know, I will ask the **mouse** to help us. **Mouse**! **Mouse**! Please help us to **pull** up the **turnip**."The **mouse** came and helped them.
They **pulled** and **pulled,** and then suddenly they **pulled** up the **turnip**. Everyone was very happy, and they all thanked the **mouse**. Everyone had **turnip soup** for dinner.

Warm-up: Enormous, Enormous Turnip. All the children except the child who is *It*, sit in a circle. *It* walks around the circle, tapping each player on the head, saying "Enormous" each time until he decides to tap someone and say "Turnip." That child becomes the turnip and runs after *It*, trying to tag him before *It* can take his seat. If *It* successfully reaches the turnip's seat without being tagged, the turnip is the new *It*. If the turnip tags *It*, then the turnip keeps his spot in the circle, and *It* must either continue to be *It* for another turn or sit in the middle of the circle until another *It* is tagged.

Circle time: Ask the children to sit in a circle. Ask them if they can name the different characters in the story. Ask the following questions:
How would they move?
What do you think they were doing before they were called to help with the Turnip?
How do they feel about pulling the turnip up and eating it?

Role-play: Get the children to find their own space in the room. When the teacher calls out a character, the children must become the character and move around the room.

Old Man: Hunches over and moves very slowly with a walking stick.

Wife: Busy doing housework and moves very busily and quickly.

Boy: Plays football, does headers, keepy-ups and scores goals.

Girl: Skips along happily.

Dog: Moves like a dog and barks.

Cat: Moves like a cat and meows.

Mouse: Moves like a mouse and squeaks.

Mime: All the children find a space and they curl up and imagine that they are a turnip seed. The seed are getting bigger and bigger until eventually, they grow into a large turnip and are pulled from the earth. They make a still image of the moment they find out that they are going to be turned into turnip soup.

Thought tracking: The teacher goes and taps each turnip on the shoulder, and they must say in one word how they feel about being eaten for dinner.

Voice production: Each child says the following sentence: "Please, please don't eat me for your dinner," in a…

- *Cheerful voice*
- *Sad voice*
- *Surprised voice*
- *Shocked voice*
- *Tired voice*
- *Angry voice*
- *Scared voice*
- *Excited voice*

Group sculpture: Divide the class into groups of 3 or 4. The group must use their bodies to make the one big, enormous turnip. They must move as the turnip but stay connected.

Teacher in role: Teacher takes the role of turnip. She must plead with the group and help persuade the woman not to make dinner with her. The group must explain to the woman why she shouldn't eat the turnip.

Freeze Frame: Divide the class into groups of 8. Each group must make six still images that tell the story. They can show it to the other groups.

Improvisation: For older children, they can add dialogue to their freeze frames.

Closure: The children stand in a circle. Child A says, "If I had a turnip, I would turn it into an apple." Child B says, "If I had a turnip, I would turn it in to an apple and a banana." Child C says, "If I had a turnip, I would turn it in to an apple, a banana and a cat," and so on until everyone gets a chance. If they make a mistake or stumble, they are eliminated and sit down. The last child standing at the end wins.

The Hare and the Tortoise

Each child finds a space and sits down. Each child or a group of children are assigned a specific word and a corresponding action. The narrator/teacher reads the story aloud, and when the children hear their word, they must jump up and do their actions. The words are in bold to assist the teacher.

Movement: Action/sound.
Boast/boastful/boasting: Stand up straight and puff out your chest.
Woods: Children make themselves into trees.
Animals: Each child chooses a different animal found in the woods and moves like that animal.
Hare: Make bunny ears with your hands.
Fast: Children move as fast as they can.
Run: Run on the spot.
Tortoise: Children bend over as if they have something heavy on their back.
Slow: Children move in slow motion around the room.

Narrator: Once upon a time, there was a very **boastful hare** that lived in the **woods** with lots of other **animals**. He was always **boasting** about how **fast** he could **run**. He **boasted,** "I'm the **fastest** animal in the woods. No one can **run** as **fast** as me." The other **animals** were tired of listening to him. One day the

tortoise said to the **hare,** "**Hare,** you are so **boastful**. I challenge you to a race." **Hare** laughed and said, "**Tortoise**, you will never beat me. You are too **slow** and steady." They decided whoever got to the other side of the **woods** the **fastest** was the winner. All the other **animals** in the **woods** came to watch the race. The **hare ran** as **fast** as he could through the **woods**. After a while, he thought to himself, "I'm so **fast** that **slow** tortoise will never beat me. I think I will take a quick nap." Soon he fell asleep. The **tortoise** walked **slowly** through the **woods**. He passed the sleeping **hare**. The **animals** watched the **tortoise** near the finishing line. The **animals** cheered loudly. The **Hare** woke up and **ran** as **fast** as he could through the **woods** to the finishing line, but it was too late. The **slow tortoise** had won the race. All the **animals** in the **woods** congratulated the **tortoise**. The **hare** had to remind himself that he shouldn't **boast** about his **fast** pace, because **slow** and steady won the race.

Warm-up: Get each child to find a clear space. They must make sure that they are not touching anyone else. The children crouch down on the floor and make a ball shape with their bodies. The teacher explains that all children are magic rocks and that the teacher is a magic wizard. The teacher waves the magic wand and says: "Magic rocks, turn into hares." All the children turn into hares and move around the room as hares. The teacher then says: "Magic rocks, turn into magic rocks." The children return to their clear spaces and crouch down on the floor again as quickly as possible. The magic wizard can change the magic rocks into any animal that can be found in the jungle.
Variation: The children can take turns being the magic wizard.

Role on the wall: Divide the class into groups of four. Give each group either an outline of the hare or the tortoise and ask the children to draw or write inside the image the different characteristics or personality traits of the hare or the tortoise. If they are too young to write, get them to draw inside the image. The teacher may also ask them what their word is and write it for them. Each group talks about their image and the words or drawings they put inside.

Still image/thought tracking: Ask each child to make a still image of the Hare at the beginning of the race. The teacher taps each child on the shoulder, and they must say how they feel. Then get them to make a still image of the hare at the end of the race. The teacher taps each child on the shoulder again, and they must say how they feel. Can they tell the difference?

Slow motion: Divide the class into pairs; one of the children is the hare and the other is the tortoise. They go to the starting line, and they are going to move in slow motion to the finishing line but showing what happened between the start of the race and the ending.
Extension: They can fast-forward or rewind.

Teacher in role: The teacher takes on the role of the tortoise. She tells the children she feels sorry for the hare because he thought he was the fastest in the forest and now he is upset. Ask the children what they suggest they could do to make him feel better.

Hot seating: One of the children volunteers to be the hare. The hare sits in the hot seat, and the rest of the children ask him questions.

Closure: The children sit in a circle. Each child finishes the following sentence: "If I could be an animal, I would be a _____."

The Lion and the Clever Rabbit

The following is a drama workshop is based on the fable from the Panchatantra called, *The Lion and the Clever Rabbit.*

The teacher can assign all the roles to the children, and the class can act out the play. Alternatively, the teacher can be the narrator and the children can play the different animals. If the children are too young to read, the teacher can read the entire the play by herself.

Characters: Three narrators, rabbit, lion, deer, elephant.

Narrator 1: Once upon a time, in a jungle in India...

Narrator 2: ...there lived a lion. He was very powerful and very cruel.

Narrator 3: He hunted and killed a lot of animals in the jungle. Sometimes, he just hunted and killed for fun.

Rabbit: We must stop this unnecessary killing.

Elephant: How can we stop the lion? He is too powerful.

Deer: Why don't we have a meeting with the lion...

Fox: ...and see if we can reach an agreement?

Narrator 1: So, all the animals in the jungle gathered together and invited the lion to the meeting.

Lion: What do you want?

Rabbit: Your Majesty, we are happy for you to be the King of the Jungle.

Deer: We are happy for you to rule the jungle.

Elephant: We understand that you need to kill us for food.

Lion: Why, that is most kind and understanding of you!

Rabbit: But you are killing animals for fun and not when you are hungry. And if you don't stop, there won't be any animals left in jungle.

Lion: Well, what do you suggest?

Rabbit: We decided that we will send you an animal a day to your den. You can kill and eat it. You won't have to go to the bother of hunting.

Lion: Well, that sounds like a good idea.

Narrator 3: The day arrived where it was the rabbits turn to go to the lion's den.

Rabbit: I don't want to go.

Other animals: You must go. If you don't go, he will kill the other animals. It was your idea.

Rabbit: I better go then.

Lion: Why are you late?

Rabbit: Your Majesty, it was not my fault. Another lion chased me; no wanted to eat me. He said he was King of the Jungle.

Lion: I'm the only King of the Jungle. Who is he? Take me to him at once. I shall kill him.

Rabbit: Come with me. I will show you where he lives.

Narrator 1: The lion followed the rabbit through the jungle.

Narrator 2: They reached a well.

Rabbit: He lives here.

Narrator 3. The lion roared and looked into the well. He saw his own reflection looking back at him.

Lion: I see him.

Rabbit: There can only be one King of the Jungle. You must kill him.

Narrator 1: The lion jumped into the well and was taken away.

(The rabbit went off and told his friends what had happened. They all had a big party to celebrate.)

Warm-up: In each group, there is a monkey, an elephant, a snake and a rabbit. Get the children to move around the room and sound like their different animals. Get them to find the animal that is like them from the other groups and interact and play with them. The teacher gives a loud roar and the animals are frightened and they return quickly to their original groups.

Teacher in role: The teacher in role as the lion roars at them. She says, "I'm very hungry and I'm going to eat all the animals in the jungle, one by one."

Still Image: In their animal groups, the children make a still image of how they feel when they think the lion is coming to get catch them and eat them.

Thought tracking: Once all groups are in the still image, then the teacher, out of role, goes and
touches them on the shoulder. Each animal has to say how they feel at that moment.

Conscience alley: Once the children are out of their still image, they make two lines facing each other. The teacher in role as the lion walks in between the line as the children speak out as his conscience. The children in the line on the left side should speak out that it is wrong to scare and eat the other animals, and the children on the right side should speak out saying that he is right to scare and eat the animals.
Examples: The left side could say, "The animals are scared." "What about their families?"
"They want to stay in the jungle and play with their friends."
The right side could say, "None of the other animals like you." "You are hungry, and you need to eat." "You have no friends, so you don't care what they think of you."

Hot seating: The teacher in role as the lion sits in the hot seat. The children who are being themselves ask the lion why he is behaving this way. Why does he want to eat all the animals in the jungle? Why is he horrible and mean to the other animals?

Group discussion: Get the children to get into role as their original animals. Tell them that they
are going to change the ending of the story because the way the clever rabbit treated the lion was as bad as how the lion treated the other animals. They must come up with a more positive ending.

Group improvisation: The groups all improvise their endings in front of the other groups. The teacher takes on the role as the lion in each group.

Role on the wall: Put two outlines of a lion on the wall. Let the children choose words that describe the lion before he got stuck in the well and one for after he was rescued from the well. The teacher can write the words in the outline.

Closure/relaxation activity: Sleeping Lions – Get the children to lie still on the floor and pretend
to be asleep. If they move, then they are out and must wake up with a loud roar.

Goldilocks and the Three Bears

Each child finds a space and sits down. Each child or a group of children are assigned a specific word and a corresponding action. The narrator/teacher reads the story aloud, and when the children hear their word, they must jump up and do their actions. The words are in bold to assist the teacher/narrator.

Movement: Action/sound.
Goldilocks: Skip around the space.
Bear/Bears: Walk slowly and growl.
Bowl/Bowls: Clasp fingers together and stick out arms to make a round shape.
Porridge: Wiggle body up and down.
Chair/s: Squat down and stick out arms.
Bed/s: Lie straight on the floor.
First: Hold up one finger.
Second: Hold up two fingers.
Third: Hold up three fingers.

Narrator: Once upon a time, there was a girl called **Goldilocks**. One day, she decided to go for a walk in the woods. Soon, she became tired. She saw a little cottage in the woods. She knocked, but there was no answer, so she decided to go inside and rest.

At the table in the kitchen, there were three **bowls** of porridge. **Goldilocks** was hungry. She tasted the **porridge** from the **first bowl**.

"This **porridge** is too hot!" she exclaimed.

So, she tasted the **porridge** from the **second bowl**.

"This **porridge** is too cold," she said.

So, she tasted the **third bowl** of **porridge**.

"Ahhh, this **porridge** is just right," she said happily, and she ate it all up.

After she'd eaten the three bears' breakfasts, she decided she was feeling a little tired. So, she walked into the living room where she saw three chairs. **Goldilocks** sat in the **first chair** to rest her feet.

"This **chair** is too big!" she exclaimed.

So, she sat in the **second chair**.

"This **chair** is too big, too!" she whined.

So, she tried the **third** and smallest **chair**.

"Ahhh, this **chair** is just right," she sighed. But just as she settled down into the **chair** to rest, it broke into pieces!

Goldilocks was very tired by this time, so she went upstairs to the bedroom. She lay down in the **first bed**, but it was too hard. Then she lay in the **second bed**, but it was too soft. Then she lay down in the **third bed**, and it was just right. **Goldilocks** fell asleep.

As she was sleeping, the three bears came home.

"Someone's been eating my **porridge**," growled Papa **bear**.

"Someone's been eating my **porridge**," said Mama **bear**.

"Someone's been eating my **porridge**, and they ate it all up!" cried Baby **bear**.

"Someone's been sitting in my **chair**," growled Papa **bear**.

"Someone's been sitting in my **chair**," said Mama **bear**.

"Someone's been sitting in my **chair**, and they've broken it all to pieces," cried Baby **bear**.

They decided to look around some more, and when they got upstairs to the bedroom, Papa **bear** growled, "Someone's been sleeping in my **bed**,"

"Someone's been sleeping in my **bed**, too," said Mama **bear**

"Someone's been sleeping in my **bed**, and she's still there!" exclaimed Baby **bear**.

Just then, Goldilocks woke up and saw the three **bears**. She screamed, "Help!" And she jumped up and ran out of the room. **Goldilocks** ran down the stairs, opened the door, and ran away into the woods. And **Goldilocks** never returned to the home of the three **bears**.

Introduction: Show the children pictures. Tell them there are 8 different types of bears. There are eight species in the bear family: Asiatic Black Bear, Brown Bear, North American Black Bear, Panda Bear, Polar Bear, Sloth Bear, Spectacled Bear, and the Sun Bear.

Warm-up: The warm-up is a movement activity called "Does a Bear Live in the Woods?"
A clear space is needed. The teacher explains to the class that when they come across a bear in the woods, they must lie down on the ground and keep very still. One child volunteers to be the bear. The bear goes to one end of the clear space and turns

his/her back on the rest of the class. All the other children try to sneak up behind the bear. When the bear turns around, all the children must lie very still on the ground. If the bear sees you moving, s/he pulls you away to join him/her. Then there are two bears. Eventually, all the children are caught moving and become bears.

Voice production: Tell the children that they are going to explore different voices. We need to change our voices to show different emotions or to become different characters.
Get the group to repeat the following lines together in their normal voices:
Who has been sitting in my chair?
Who has eating my porridge?
Who has been sleeping in my bed?

Now, get the children to say the lines in the following ways:

Loud

Quiet

Fast

Slow

Sad

Happy

Angry

Excited

Surprised

Frightened

Annoyed

Role-play: "Now we are going to warm up our bodies. Everyone find a space and walk around the room as yourself. When I say freeze, I will call out different ways of walking…."

Walk as
Papa bear
Mama bear
Baby bear
Goldilocks
Grumpy Papa bear
Kind Mama bear
Happy Baby bear
Surprised Goldilocks

Sculpting: Divide the class into pairs: one person is the sculptor the other is the clay. Get the sculptor to mold the clay into…
How did Goldilocks feel when the bears found her?
How did Baby bear feel when he saw that his porridge had been eaten?
How did Mama bear feel when she saw that someone had been sleeping in her bed?
How Papa bear feel when he saw Goldilocks sleeping in the bed?
It can be abstract. The teacher/children look at each sculpture and guess how the characters are feeling.

Movement poem: Teach the children the following poem and actions.

When Goldilocks Went to the House of the Bears

When Goldilocks went to the house of the bears *(the children walk on the spot)*, oh, what did her blue eyes see? *(The children point to their eyes.)* A bowl that was huge and a bowl that was small and a bowl that was tiny and that was all. *(Children make increasingly smaller shapes with their arms to represent each bowl.)* And she counted them – one, two, three! *(They use one finger to point, as if counting each bowl.)* When Goldilocks went to the house of the bears *(walk on the spot)*, oh, what did her blue eyes see? *(Point to their eyes.)* A chair that was huge and a chair that was small, and a chair that was tiny and that was all. *(Use hands to show the different heights and the size of each chair, getting smaller all the time.)* And she counted them – one, two, three! *(Use their fingers to point, as if counting each chair.)* When Goldilocks went to the house of the bears *(walk on the spot)*, oh, what did her blue eyes see? *(Point to their eyes.)* A bed that was huge and a bed that was small and a bed that was tiny and that was all. *(Use their hands to show the increasingly smaller length and size of each bed.)* And she counted them – one, two, three! *(Use their fingers to point, as if counting each bed.)* When Goldilocks went to the house of the bears *(walk on the spot)*, oh, what did her blue eyes see? *(Point to their eyes.)* A bear that was huge and a bear that was small and a bear that was tiny and that was all. *(Use hands to show the increasingly smaller height and size of each bear.)*

Closure/the bears are coming: The teacher tells the children, "Before we had the internet, cars, computers, trains, planes, washing machines, and hoovers, people had to chop wood. Talk about type of jobs people did in the olden days." All the children must find some physical action, based on an old-fashioned job like wood chopping, hunting, or washing clothes, and begin doing this action somewhere in the room. The teacher/volunteer leaves the room momentarily and returns as the bear. Once the bear arrives, the children must freeze where they are, and the bear must try to make the other children laugh. If a child laughs, they become a bear and the bears work together until they have made everyone laugh. The bears cannot touch the frozen children!

The Lion and the Mouse

Each child finds a space and sits down. Each child or a group of children are assigned a specific word and a corresponding action. The narrator/teacher reads the story aloud, and when the children hear their word, they must jump up and do their actions. The words are in bold to assist the teacher/narrator.

Movement: Action/sound.
Lion: Get down on hands and knees and move around stealthily as a lion stalking his prey.
Mouse: Scamper like a mouse and squeak.
Forest: Make yourself into a large tree.
Roar/roared/roaring: Roar loudly like a lion.
Eat: Do a gobbling action.
Help: Extend hands in a kindly gesture.

Narrator: One day, a **lion** was fast asleep in the **forest**. His head rested on his paw and he was snoring away. A timid little **mouse** came scampering by him and accidentally scampered across the **lion's** nose. The lion woke up with a loud **roar**. The **lion** laid his huge paw angrily on the timid little **mouse**. He **roared**, "I'm going to **eat** you up."

"Don't **eat** me!" begged the poor **mouse**. "Please let me go and someday I will **help** you."

The **lion** was much amused to think that a **mouse** could ever **help** him. But he was generous and finally let the **mouse** go.

Some days later, while walking in the **forest**, the **lion** was caught in a hunter's net. Unable to free himself, he filled the **forest** with his angry **roaring**. The **mouse** heard the roar and quickly found the **lion** trapped in the net. Running to one of the great ropes that bound him, she chewed it until it fell apart, and soon the **lion** was free.

"You laughed when I said one day, I would **help** you," said the **mouse**. "Now, you see that even a **mouse** can help a **lion**."

They hugged, and from then on, the **lion** and the **mouse** were very good friends.

Introduction:

Ask the children to name different jungle animals. They discuss what they can do, what they eat, where they live in the jungle. Then each child chooses their favorite jungle animal. The teacher goes around the circle and each child get an opportunity to speak about its favorite jungle animal

My favorite animal is …..
It's …….
It's got……..
It lives in………
It eats …….
It moves like………..

Warm-up: Children are running through the "jungle" and run into many animals, etc. that they need to get away from. The teacher can give appropriate commands, and the children carry out a suitable action such as:

Jump over logs.
Duck under branches.
High knees through quicksand.
Run from the tiger.
Tip toe past the snake.
Talk to the monkeys (ooh, ooh, aah, aah).

Teacher in role: The Lion's Court: Before starting this game, it is a good idea for the teacher to talk about the different animals that are found in the jungle. The teacher should ask the children, "Who is the King of the Jungle?" The teacher then assumes the role of a lion who is the King of the Jungle. It would be a good idea to have a crown for the lion. The children can make a court for the lion with chairs and a table or with cushions. Inside the court, the lion sits on a throne. Each child chooses an animal they would like to pretend to be. The lion tells the other animals he is looking for animals to join his court. One by one he calls all the animals to him and asks them why he should let them join his court. The child must say what type of animal they are and what good qualities they have and how they will be useful to the lion, the King of the Jungle. When they have finished, the King says, "You may join my court," and lets them in. This is why it is a good idea to have a designated area in the jungle.

Closure: Sleeping Lions: All the children are lions (tigers, cows or any animal they want to be). They lie down on the floor; eyes closed and stay still, as if they were sleeping. The teacher goes around the room, trying to get the lions to move. If they move, then they must get up and help the teacher to try to get the other lions to move. They are not allowed to touch the lions, but may move close to them, tell jokes or make faces. After five minutes, with a loud roar, tell the lions who are still on the floor to wake up.

The Three Little Pigs

Each child finds a space and sits down. Each child or a group of children are assigned a specific word and a corresponding action. The narrator/teacher reads the story aloud and when the children hear their word they must jump up and do their actions. The words are in bold to assist the teacher/narrator.

Movement: Action/sound.
Any number: Show that number of fingers.
Little: Crouch down as small as you can.
Pig: Get on all fours and oink once.
Pigs: Get on all fours and oink twice.
Big: Stretch up as high as you can.
Bad: Make an angry face.
Wolf: Make hands into claws and say "aargh."
Laughing: Laugh loudly.
Smiling: Give a big wide smile.
Trotted: Trot up and down the space.
Straw: Rub your hands together.
Sticks: Clap your hands together.
Bricks: Clap your hands on your thighs.
Huff/huffed: Blow.
Puff/puffed: Blow harder.
Blow/blew: Stamp feet on the ground.

Narrator: Once upon a time, there was a mother **pig** who lived with her **three little pigs**. One day she said, "**Little pigs,** I think it is time for you to leave and make your own way in this **big** world. You each need to build your own **house**." The little pigs were very excited about their new, **big** adventure. Mother **pig** gave each of her **little pigs** a hug, but she warned them, "Remember to watch out for the **big bad wolf**." The **little pigs** waved goodbye to their mother, and they **trotted** into the woods. They were **laughing** and **smiling,** and soon they came across a man who was carrying some **straw**. The **first little pig** said, "May I have some **straw** to build my **house**?" The man said kindly, "Of course, you may." The man gave the **first little pig** some **straw** to build his house. Just before they left, the man warned them, "Watch out for the **big bad wolf**." The **first little pig** built his **house** of **straw**.

The **two** other **pigs trotted** on down the road. They were **laughing** and **smiling,** and soon they came across a man who was carrying some **sticks**. The **second little pig** said, "May I have some **sticks** to build my **house**?" The man said kindly, "Of course, you may." The man gave the **second** little **pig** some **sticks** to build his house. Just before they left, the man warned them, "Watch out for the **big bad wolf**." The **second little pig** built his **house** of **sticks**.

The **third little pig trotted** on down the road. He was laughing and **smiling,** and soon he came across a man who was carrying some **bricks**. The third little pig said, "May I have some **bricks** to build my house?" The man said kindly, "Of course, you may." The man gave the **third little pig** some **bricks** to build his **house**. Just before they left, the man warned him, "Watch out for the **big bad wolf**."

The **third** little **pig** built his **house** of **bricks**. The **first little pig** had just finished building his **house** of **straw** when the **big bad wolf** appeared. He said, **"Little pig, little pig**, let me come in."
The **first little pig** replied, "Not by the hair of my chinny, chin, chin."
Then the **wolf** said, Then I'll **huff,** and I'll **puff,** and I will **blow** the **house** down." So, he **huffed,** and he **puffed,** and he **blew** the **house** down.
The **first little pig trotted** very quickly to his brother's **house** made of **sticks**. The **second** little **pig** had just finished building his **house** of **sticks** when he heard a knock on the door, and to his surprise, it was his brother. Suddenly, the **big bad wolf** appeared.
He said, **"Little pig, little pig**, let me come in."
The **second little pig** replied, "Not by hair of my chinny, chin, chin."
Then the **wolf** said, "Then I'll **huff,** and I'll **puff,** and I will **blow** the house down." So, he **huffed,** and he **puffed,** and he **blew** the **house** down.
The **two** little **pigs trotted** very quickly to their brother's house made of **bricks**.
The **third little pig** had just finished building his **house** of **bricks** when he heard a knock on the door, and to his surprise, it was his **two** brothers. Suddenly, the **big bad wolf** appeared. He said, "**Little pig, little pig**, let me come in."
The **third** little **pig** replied, "Not by hair of my chinny, chin, chin."
Then the **wolf** said, "Then I'll **huff,** and I'll **puff,** and I will **blow** the **house** down." The wolf **huffed,** and he **puffed**. He **huffed,** and he **puffed,** but he couldn't **blow** the **house** down.

He heard the **three little pigs** inside the **house**. They were **laughing**. This made the **wolf** very angry indeed. He decided he would climb to the top of the roof and come down the chimney.

The **third little pig** heard him on the roof, and he came up with a clever plan. He put a **big** pot of boiling water on the fire, which was just underneath the chimney. The **wolf** came tumbling down the chimney and landed into the **big** pot of boiling water and "SPLASH!" That was the end of the **big bad wolf**. The **three little pigs** lived happily ever after.

Warm-up: One child is chosen or volunteers to be Mr. or Ms. Wolf and stands at one side of the clear space. His/her back is to the other children, who are standing at the opposite end of the space. The rest of the children shout out: "What's the time, Mr. /Ms. Wolf?" The wolf does not turn around. He/she replies in a rough, wolf-like voice: "Four o'clock." The children walk forward the number of steps the wolf calls out (in this case, four). The children ask again: "What time is it, Mr./Ms. Wolf?" The wolf replies: "Five o'clock." The children take five steps forward. The children continue to ask the question and to walk the appropriate number of steps forward. Eventually, when the wolf thinks that the children are near enough, he/she will say: "Dinnertime!" Then the wolf turns around and chases the children. They must try to rush back to their starting place. If Mr./Ms. Wolf catches one of them before they reach home, that child is the wolf in the next game.

Choral speaking: Teach the children the following poem. Get them to think of different actions for the straw, sticks, bricks, pigs and wolf. They say the poem in unison.

Straw, Sticks and Bricks
Straw, sticks and bricks.
Straw, sticks and bricks.
The pigs built their houses
Out of straw, sticks and bricks

The wolf came by,
He blew the straw down.
He blew the sticks, but the bricks were strong
The pig lived happy all the days long
In their house of bricks.

Occupational mime: Divide the class into groups of 4: three pigs and one wolf. The pigs move round the room in a "follow the leader" style. The pig at the front of the line is doing the actions. The first pig mimes collecting materials and building a house of straw. Second and third pigs follow, copying the mime. When the house is blown down by the wolf, the first pig moves to the end of the line. Second pig then heads the line and mimes building house of sticks. Finally, third pig takes a turn and mimes building a house of bricks. The wolf moves around the room avoiding pigs as they build until it is time to blow the house down.

Role-play: Encourage different movements such as gathering straw, breaking sticks or lifting heavy bricks. Encourage the wolves to use their body and facial expression to look fierce and threatening. Give everyone in the group the opportunity to take on the role of the wolf. When the children are comfortable with the character movements, get them to use speech. Ask the following questions:

What does the wolf sound like?
What would he say to the little pigs?
What do the pigs sound like?
What would they say to the wolf?

Talking objects: Ask children if they can take on the role of the wolf. They use their breath to blow down the house. Get them to huff and puff and huff and puff and blow the house down. Everyone sits in a circle and the teacher presents the group with objects that can be blown down by the breath, the wind or a hurricane such as a leaf, balloon, paper, tree, car or even a bridge. Every child becomes an object; they enter the circle and give the group some information about who they are. For example: "I'm small, I'm green and live on a tree." Once the rest of group have guessed correctly, everyone blows the object down.

Conclusion: The teacher discusses with the group reasons why the wolf gets very angry. The teacher asks the children how they can show the wolf how to relax using his breath. The wolf uses his breath to blow things down, but he could use his breath for relaxation exercises.

Tummy breathing: The children find their own space on the floor. They lie down and place their hands or a stuffed toy on their tummy. They inhale on a count of three. They see their hands or stuffed toy rising as their tummy fills with air. They exhale on the count of four and they see their hands or stuffed toys falling. Repeat this process 10 times. When everyone is finished, ask the children the following questions:

How do you feel?

What did you notice about your hands/stuffed toy when you inhaled and exhaled?

How would this exercise help the wolf?

Burst balloon: The children all lie on the floor. The teacher gets them to imagine that their body is a balloon. They are going to close their eyes and inflate the balloon. They fill up their tummies with air. Then when they are full, the teacher counts to three and the children shout bang and they let all the air out of their bodies like a deflated balloon.

The Little Red Hen

Each child finds a space and sits down. Each child or a group of children are assigned a specific word and a corresponding action. The narrator/teacher reads the story aloud, and when the children hear their word, they must jump up and do their actions. The words are in bold to assist the teacher/narrator.

Movement: Action/sound.
Little Red Hen: Make yourself as small as possible and cluck around like a chicken.
Plant: Mime digging a hole and planting a seed.
Wheat: Make your body into the shape of a wheat plant.
Dogs: Move and bark like a dog.
Ducks: Waddle and quack like a duck.
Geese: Move like a goose and say "gobble, gobble."
Cats: Move like a cat and meow.
Cut: Use a slashing movement.
Bread and cakes: Mime eating a delicious cake.

Once upon a time, there was a **little red hen** that lived on a farm. She was always busy! She spent all morning laying eggs for the farmer.

"**Little Red Hen**, please lay an egg for my tea," said the farmer. After the **little red hen** had laid her egg, she found a grain of wheat. She wanted to **plant** it in a field.

"I'll ask my animal friends to help me. **Dogs, Dogs**! Will you help me **plant** the **wheat?**" she said.

"Oh no, we will not help you. We are too busy burying our bones. Get the **ducks** to help you," barked the **dogs**.

"**Ducks, Ducks**! Will you help me **plant** the **wheat?**" said the **little red hen.**

"Oh no, we will not help you. We are too busy swimming. Get the **geese** to help you," quacked the **ducks**.

"**Geese, Geese**! Will you help me **plant** the **wheat?**" said the **little red hen.**

"Oh no, we will not help you. We are too busy sunbathing. Get the **cats** to help you," gaggled the **geese**.

"**Cats, Cats**! Will you help me **plant** the **wheat?**" said the **little red hen.**

"Oh no, we will not help you. **Plant** it yourself," meowed the **cats**.

No one would help the **little red hen,** so she **planted** it herself. The sun and the rain helped the **wheat** to grow. Soon, the **wheat** was tall and yellow and needed to be **cut**. "I'll ask my animal friends to help me. **Dogs, Dogs**! Will you help me **cut** the **wheat?**" said the **little red hen.**

"Oh no, we will not help you. We are too busy burying our bones. Get the **ducks** to help you," barked the **dogs**.

"**Ducks, Ducks**! Will you help me **cut** the **wheat?**" said the **little red hen.**

"Oh no, we will not help you. We are too busy swimming. Get the **geese** to help you," **quacked** the **ducks**.

"Geese, Geese! Will you help me cut the wheat?" said the **little red hen.**

"Oh no, we will not help you. We are too busy sunbathing. Get the **cats** to help you," gaggled the **geese**.

"**Cats, Cats**! Will you help me cut the wheat?" said the **little red hen**.
"Oh no, we will not help you. We are too busy washing our faces. **Cut** it yourself," meowed the cats.
So, the **little red hen cut** the **wheat** herself, and she took the **wheat** to the miller. The miller turned the **wheat** into flour.
"Here's your flour to make **bread and cakes**," said the miller.
The **little red hen** thanked the miller. She made **bread and cakes**.
"Who will help me eat the **bread and cakes**?" said the **little red hen**.
"We will!" shouted all the animals.
"Oh no, I will eat it myself. If you want to eat the food, what will you do next time?" asked the **little red hen**.
"We will share the work," said all the animals.

Warm-up: The teacher asks the children to take on the role of animals found on a farm and to make a noise that sounds like their animal. They move around the room as their animal. Eventually, everyone sits in a circle and the teacher asks them to make each noise individually and then brings them together to make a farmyard morning chorus.

Teacher in role: The teacher takes on the role of the little red hen. The children ask her questions in role about how she was feeling at various parts of the story.

Sample questions:
How would you describe the cat, the goose, and the dog?
What words can you use to describe yourself?
How do you feel doing all the work by yourself?

How do you feel when all the animals wanted to eat the bread she had made?
Why did you say the other animals could not eat the bread?
How do you think the animals felt when you told them they could not help to eat the bread?
What lesson did the animals learn? Do you think they will be more willing to help next time? Why or why not?
How would the story be different if all the animals had agreed to help the little red hen with the work?

Hot seating: The children choose to be either the dog or cat or pig. Each child takes it in turns to sit in the hot seat as their characters. The rest of the children ask the character in the hot seat characters.
Sample questions:
Why are you so lazy?
Why didn't you help the little red hen?
Do you think you are right in not helping her?
Do you think the little red hen should share with you?
How did you feel when the little red hen wouldn't share the bread with you?
Do you think the ending of the story would be different if you had agreed to help the little red hen?

Movement Song: The little red hen song is sung to the tune of, "This is the way we brush our teeth, so early in the morning."
This is the way I plant the seed, plant the seed, plant the seed.
This is the way I plant the seed, so early in the morning.
(Everyone mimes digging a hole and planting a seed.)

This is the way I water the wheat. water the wheat, water the wheat. This the way I water the wheat, so early in the morning. *(Everyone mimes watering the wheat with a watering can.)* This is the way I cut the wheat. cut the wheat, cut the wheat. This the way I cut the wheat, so early in the morning. *(Everyone mimes chopping down the wheat with a knife.)* This is the way I go to the mill, go to the mill, go to the mill. This the way I go to the mill so early in the morning. *(Everyone mimes walking to the mill with a bag on their back.)* This is the way I make the dough. make the dough, make the dough. This the way I make the dough, so early in the morning. *(Everyone mime kneading the dough.)* This is the way I bake the bread, bake the bread, bake the bread. This the way I bake the bread, so early in the morning. *(Everyone mimes putting the bread in the oven.)* This is the way I eat the bread, eat the bread, eat the bread. This the way I eat the bread, so early in the morning. *(Everyone mimes eating the bread.)*

Sculpts: The teacher places baking tools or pictures of baking tools inside a box, such as a rolling pin, measuring cup and spoons, spatula, wooden spoon, cookie cutters, bowl, etc. Each child comes to the box and takes out one item. Let each of the children hold the item. Name the item and discuss what each tool is used for. Place the item in the middle of the circle. Continue until all children have had a turn. Then, they use their body to make the shape of the baking tool. At the end, everyone could make a group sculpture of what is found in a baking drawer.

Extensions: Choose four to five items. Ask the children to cover their eyes and remove one item. They must guess the missing tool. Ask the children to cover their eyes. Place one item inside the box. Invite one child to feel the item inside the box without looking. What tool is inside the box?

Still image: Put the children into small groups and ask them to recreate a scene from the story through a still image. Encourage the children to use their imagination and take on the roles of inanimate objects, like the corn and the windmill. The groups show their still image to the other groups. The rest of the children must guess what is happening in the still images.

Role-play: Ask the children to try and act out the story using animal masks and encourage them to act like their animal by making the noises associated with it and walking like it.

Perceive and reflect: Everyone sits in a circle and the teacher recalls a story where she remembered a time when someone helped her with something difficult. She asks the children to share their stories about doing something difficult by themselves. The teacher then remembers a time when she had to do something difficult all by herself. She invites the children to talk about their stories where they had to something difficult by themselves. The teacher remembers a time where she helped someone with a difficult job, and it made it heaps easier for them. She invites the children to talk about their stories when they helped someone do something difficult.

Chicken Licken

Each child finds a space and sits down. Each child or a group of children are assigned a specific word and a corresponding action. The narrator/teacher reads the story aloud, and when the children hear their word, they must jump up and do their actions. The words are in bold to assist the teacher.

Word: Action/sound.
Chicken Licken: Bawk, bawk/walks around looking confused.
Henny Penny: Cluck, cluck/flap wings very fast.
Cocky Locky: Cock-a-doodle-doo/curl your body into a ball and then stretch up as high as you can.
Ducky Lucky: Quack, quack/waddle from side to side.
Drakey Lakey: Squeak, squeak/swims in the water.
Goosey Loosey: Honk, honk/pecks at the ground looking for food.
Turkey Lurkey: Gobble, gobble, gobble/puff your chest and strut forward and backwards.
Foxy Loxy: Say, "I've got a cunning plan."/move slowly and stealthy.
King: Say, "Yes, your majesty"/bow.
Sky: Say, "Help, help."/fall on the ground

Once upon a time, there was a chicken called **Chicken Licken** who lived on a farmyard with lots of other animals. One day,

Chicken Licken was flapping his wings when suddenly an acorn fell from an oak tree. *Plonk!* It hit **Chicken Licken** on the head. OUCH! Unfortunately, **Chicken Licken** didn't see the acorn. He looked up at **sky**. "Oh, no!" he said, "The **sky** is falling down. I must tell the **king**." On his way to tell the **king**, he met **Henny Penny**.

"Where are you going in such a hurry?" clucked **Henny Penny**.
"The **sky** is falling down and I'm going to tell the **king**," cried **Chicken Licken**.
"I'll come too," clucked **Henny Penny**. So, **Chicken Licken** and **Henny Penny** went off to tell the **king** that the **sky** was falling down.
"Where are you going, in such a hurry?" crowed **Cocky Locky**.
"The **sky** is falling down we are off to tell the **king**," cried **Chicken Licken**
"I'll come too," crowed **Cocky Locky**.
So, **Chicken Licken, Henny Penny** and **Cocky Locky** went off to tell the **king** that the **sky** was falling down.
"Where are you going in such a hurry?" quacked **Ducky Lucky** and **Drakey Lakey**.
"The sky is falling down, and we are off to tell the king," cried **Chicken Licken**.
"We will come too," quacked **Ducky Lucky** and **Drakey Lakey**. So, **Chicken Licken, Henny Penny, Cocky Locky, Ducky Lucky** and **Drakey Lakey** went off to tell the **king** that the **sky** was falling down.
"Where are you going in such a hurry?" honked **Goosey Loosey**.
"The **sky** is falling down, and we are off to tell the **king**," cried **Chicken Licken**.
"I'll come too," honked **Goosey Loosey**.

So, **Chicken Licken, Henny Penny, Cocky Locky, Ducky Lucky, Drakey Lakey** and **Goosey Loosey** went off to tell the **king** that the **sky** was falling down.

"Where are you going in such a hurry?" gobbled **Turkey Lurkey**.

"The **sky** is falling, and we are off to tell the **king**," cried **Chicken Licken**.

"I'll come too," gobbled **Turkey Lurkey**. So, **Chicken Licken, Henny Penny, Cocky Locky, Ducky Lucky, Drakey Lakey, Goosey Loosey** and **Turkey Lurkey** went off to tell the **king** that the **sky** was falling down.

"Where are you going in such a hurry?" snapped **Foxy Loxy**.

"The **sky** is falling down, and we are off to tell the **king**," cried **Chicken Licken**.

"Follow me, my feathery friends. I can help you find the **king**," smiled **Foxy Loxy**.

So, **Chicken Licken, Henny Penny, Cocky Locky, Ducky Lucky, Dray Lakey, Goosey Loosey** and **Turkey Lurkey** followed **Foxy Loxy** deeper into the forest. **Foxy Loxy** was just getting ready to have a big feathery dinner when suddenly an acorn dropped from the tree. *Plonk!* And hit **Foxy Loxy** on the head. OUCH! **Foxy Loxy** didn't see the acorn. He looked up at the **sky**. "Oh, no!" he said, "The **sky** is falling down. I must tell the **king**." Foxy Loxy ran off to tell the **king** the sky was falling down.

Everyone looked at **Chicken Licken**. "Are you sure the **sky** fell on your head?" they said.

"Well, maybe it was an acorn!" said **Chicken Licken**. And they chased him all the way home to the farmyard.

Warm-up: The warm-up game is Chick, Chick, Chicken. Show the children a balloon. and tell them it is a rotten egg. Get the children to sit in a tight circle, with their hands behind their backs. One child sits in the centre of the circle and closes his/her eyes. The child in the centre of the circle is the detective. The teacher walks around the room and puts the rotten egg into one of the children's hands. The detective opens his/her eyes. The rotten egg should be passed around the circle, behind the children's backs, without the detective seeing it. The detective has three goes at guessing who has the rotten egg.

Sound collage: The children are going to imagine what it is like if the sky was falling. They are going to use their body to create the sound. Musical instruments or objects can also be used to create the sound. The first child starts, and after a few seconds, the next child joins in and then the next and then next until there is collective sound. By the time everyone has joined in, the sound should be very loud.

Movement/role-play: Ask the children to think of all the different animals in the story. Think of a new character who the animals could tell about the sky falling down. Make a new page to add to the book that includes your character. Introduce other animals that are not in the story, such as cat, frog, mouse, and snake. Ask the children to come up with a rhyming name for each of the animals, such as Catty Scatty, Foggy Logy, Snake Wakey, Mousie Wousie, etc. Discuss how each animal moves and what noise it makes. Talk about the different shapes and sizes of the animals and how they have different bodies and make different noises. Together decide on a noise and an action for each animal. Everyone walks around the room. When the teacher calls out an animal from either the story or another animal that the children come up with, they must move and sound like that animal.

Storytelling: Get the children to create a story path. The teacher gets a long sheet of paper, which is a hand-drawn path with various images from the story of Chicken Licken on it. The children take turns traveling along a path and telling the story. They can tell the story of Chicken Licken or if they wish, they could make up the story as they go. Alternatively, the children can help create the path. The teacher can discuss the important elements of the story and decide on appropriate images or cues for a group decision. They can also include some of the new characters they introduced in the previous movement activity.

Role on the wall: Work with the class to create a role on the wall for Chicken Licken. Draw an outline to represent Chicken Licken. In the space outside of the outline, write down what children notice about the character – what the character does, how she appears, what she says. Within the outline, write down words and phrases to describe the internal characteristics: words to describe her personality, as well as her thoughts and feelings. Give children the opportunity to verbalise why they believe she might be thinking or feeling those things, explicitly making the link between the external and internal behaviours and responses. How does what a character might do or say inform us about what she might be thinking or feeling? If the children are too young to write, they could draw, or the teacher could write in the words for them. They can also create a role on the wall for Foxy Loxy. When both role on the walls are finished, they can compare the two characters.

Choral speaking: The teacher introduces "The Five Little Chickens" poem. Divide the children into groups and get each group to say one verse.

Five Little Chickens
Said the first little chicken,
With a strange little squirm,
"I wish I could find
A fat little worm."

Said the second little chicken,
With an odd little shrug,
"I wish I could find
A fat little bug."

Said the third little chicken,
With a sharp little squeal,
"I wish I could find
Some nice yellow meal."

Said the fourth little chicken,
With a sigh of grief,
"I wish I could find
A little green leaf."

Said the fifth little chicken,
With a faint little moan,
"I wish I could find
A wee gravel stone."

"Now see here," said the mother,
From the green garden patch,
"If you want any breakfast,
Just come here and SCRATCH!"

Broken telephone: Chicken Licken gave the wrong message to the other animals. Broken telephone shows what can happen if a message gets mixed up. Everyone sits in a circle. The teacher whispers a word or a phrase to one child. The child passes on the message to the next child in the circle. The whispering child must make sure that they are very quiet so only the child they are passing the message to can hear them. The passing of the message is passed on around the circle, from child to child, until it reaches the last child, who calls out the message he or she received. The message at the end should be the same as the message at the beginning, but that usually doesn't happen, which leads to lots of laughter. The teacher can go around the circle and find out where the telephone line was broken.

Closure: Play the chicken song and everyone dances to it.

The Ants and the Grasshopper

Each child finds a space and sits down. Each child or a group of children are assigned a specific word and a corresponding action. The narrator/teacher reads the story aloud, and when the children hear their word, they must jump up and do their actions. The words are in bold to assist the teacher/narrator.

Word: Action/sound.
Ants: Mimes carrying something very heavy on their backs.
Grasshopper: Hopping up and down very excitedly.
Owls: Flapping their wings and saying, "Twit tu hoo."
Bears: Wake up and growl.
Squirrels: Mimes eating their nuts.
Winter/cold or colder: Whole body shivers.
Summer/hot or hotter: Wipes the sweat off their brow.
Feed: Mime eating food.

One hot summer's day, there were some **ants** working hard. They were collecting food for the winter. "We are so **hot**. This is hard work," said the **ants.**

The **ants** saw a **grasshopper** listening to some music on his iPhone. He was dancing and laughing and enjoying the lovely weather. "**Ants** you are so silly. You need to enjoy the sunshine," said the **grasshopper.**

"We are working hard. We want to have food for the **winter,**" the **ants** replied.

The **grasshopper** continued enjoying himself. **Winter** started to come, and the weather got **colder** and **colder.** The snow began to fall. The **grasshopper** was **cold** and hungry. The **grasshopper** shivered and looked up at the **owls** above. "I am **cold** and hungry; perhaps my friends the **owls** will feed me. **Owls! Owls!** Will you please **feed** me?"

The **Owls** flew down from their tree and said ,"Twit Tuhooo! Oh no, we will not **feed** you."

"Oh dear! I know," said the **grasshopper.** "I will ask my friends the **bears** to **feed** me. **Bears! Bears!** Please feed me," roared the **grasshopper.**

The **bears** were upset because they were asleep for the **winter** and the **grasshopper** woke them up. "Growl! Growl! Oh no, we will not **feed** you," said the **bears** angrily.

Then the **grasshopper** saw some **squirrels. "Squirrels! Squirrels!** Please **feed** me," said the **grasshopper.**

"Oh no, we will not **feed** you," said the **squirrels.**

The **grasshopper** was very **cold** and hungry. He didn't know what to do. Then he thought of the ants. "**Ants! Ants!** Please feed me," said the **grasshopper.**

The **ants** thought about it and decided to give him some food. "You must promise that next year you will work hard in the **summer,**" said the **ants.**

"Oh thank you, **Ants,** I promise."

That **summer,** the grasshopper kept his promise and worked hard to collect food for the next **winter.** The lesson of the story is, if you fail to prepare, you prepare to fail.

Hot seating: One of the children chooses to be in the hot-seat and assumes the role of the ant. The other children ask him questions.
Sample questions:
How did you feel when you were working hard while the grasshopper was singing and dancing?
What was it like to work as part of a team?
How did it feel to be prepared for winter?
What did you think about grasshopper when he was asking for help?
How did you feel about sharing your food from all of your hard work?
Another child volunteers to sit in the hot seat and assumes the role of the grasshopper. The other children ask questions.
Sample questions:
While you were enjoying the beauty of the summer, how did you feel when the ants kept pestering you about collecting food for the winter?
How did you feel when winter rolled around, and you had no food to eat?
What was it like to feel so cold that you had trouble speaking?
How did it make you feel when the ants saved you and brought you to their home?
What would you have done if the ants had not saved you?

Voice production: The children divide into pairs. One child is the grasshopper and the other child is the ant. Get them to experiment with their voices. How would a grasshopper sound? Maybe enthusiastic, excited, high-pitched and fast. How would an ant sound? Maybe boring, dull, low-pitched and slow.

Role-play: Once they find the characters' voices, they role-play the scene where the grasshopper asks the ant for food and the scolds him for not working during the summer.

Movement song: Teach the children the melody of the song "The Ants Go Marching." Invite the children to create movements to dramatize the different actions in each verse. Have them tap their hands on the floor when they come to the *Boom! Boom! Boom!* Select ten children to be the ants. Have the rest of the class sing the verses while the ten students dramatize the ants' movements. Take turns so all the children have an opportunity to participate in the dramatization.

The Ants Go Marching
The ants came marching one by one, Hurrah! Hurrah!
The ants came marching one by one, Hurrah! Hurrah!
The ants came marching one by one
The little one stopped to suck his thumb.
They all go marching down around the town.
Boom, Boom, Boom.
The ants came marching two by two, Hurrah! Hurrah!
The ants came marching two by two, Hurrah! Hurrah!
The ants came marching two by two
The little one stopped to tie his shoe.
They all go marching down around the town.
Boom, Boom, Boom.

The ants came marching three by three...
The little one stopped to climb a tree.

The ants came marching four by four....
The little one stopped to shut the door....
The ants came marching five by five...
The little one stopped to take a dive...
The ants came marching six by six....
The little one stopped to pick up sticks....
The ants came marching seven by seven....
The little one stopped to say 'my heaven'...
The ants came marching eight by eight...
The little one stopped to shut the gate...
The ants came marching nine by nine...
The little one stopped to scratch his spine...
The ants came marching ten by ten
The little one stopped to say THE END!

Role-play: This activity simulates the growth and change through the seasons. The children close their eyes and imagine that they are seeds growing into plants. The children lie on the floor curled up in a ball and imagine they are a seed. Ask them to move, change, and grow into a plant. The teacher gives the following instructions. Imagine you are trees blowing in a summer breeze. Then, autumn leaves are falling, whirling and twirling from the trees. Along come the ants collecting food for their winter bounty. Soon, winter comes and snowflakes gently falling from the sky. It becomes so cold icicles appear on tree branches. It starts to snow and the snow whirls in the wind. Ants in their houses enjoying the fruits of their labour. Hibernating animals going to sleep for the winter. You could include music with different tempos to help create the atmosphere.

The Three Billy Goats Gruff

Each child finds a space and sits down. Each child or a group of children are assigned a specific word and a corresponding action. The narrator/teacher reads the story aloud, and when the children hear their word, they must jump up and do their actions. The words are in bold to assist the teacher.

Movement: Action/sound.
Billy goats gruff: Move like a goat and say triplet trip.
Bridge: Two children face each other; they place their arms over their heads and link their fingers together.
Troll: Roar and make an ugly face.
Smallest: Make your body as small as you can.
Middle-sized: Stand up straight.
Bigger/Biggest: Stretch your hands up in the air as high as you can.
Meadow: Get down on your hands and knees and graze on the grass.
Hungry: Rub your tummy.
Brother: Two children link arms.
Brothers: Three children link arms.
Eat: Mime gobbling food.

Narrator: Once upon a time, there lived three **billy goats gruff.** They spent every winter in a barn that kept them nice and warm. But when the summer came, they liked to trippety trip over the **bridge** to the beautiful green **meadow** on the other side of the river. "I'm really **hungry**. I think I will cross the **bridge** to eat some lovely green grass in the **meadow**," said the **smallest billy goat gruff**.

What the **billy goats gruff** didn't know was that under the **bridge**, there lived an ugly **troll**. The **troll** was nasty and horrible.

Nobody crossed the **bridge** without the **troll's** permission, and he never gave permission.

"I can't wait to get to the **meadow**," said the **smallest billy goat gruff**.

"Who is that trippety tripping over my **bridge**?" roared the **troll**.

"Oh, it's only me. Please let me pass. I only want to go to the **meadow** to **eat** some sweet grass," pleaded the **smallest billy goat gruff**.

"Oh no, you are not. I'm going to **eat** you," said the **troll**.

"Oh, no, please, Mr. **Troll**, I'm only the **smallest billy goat gruff**. I'm much too tiny for you to **eat**, and I wouldn't taste very good. Why don't you wait for my **brother**, the **middle-sized billy goat gruff**? He is much **bigger** than I am and would be much tastier," said the **smallest billy goat gruff**.

"Well, I suppose I could wait," the **troll** said with a sigh.

"I think I will join my **brother** on the meadow and eat some lovely lush grass," mused the **middle-sized billy goats gruff**.

"Who is that trippety tripping over my **bridge**?" roared the **troll**.

"Oh, it's only me. Please let me pass. I only want to go to the **meadow** to **eat** some sweet grass" said the **middle-sized billy goat gruff**.

"Oh no, you are not. I'm going to **eat** you," bellowed the **troll**.

"Oh, no, please, Mr. **Troll**, I'm only the **middle-sized billy goat gruff**. I'm much too tiny for you to **eat,** and I wouldn't taste very good. Why don't you wait for my **brother**, the **biggest billy goat gruff**? He is much **bigger** than I am and would be much tastier," pleased the **middle-sized billy goat gruff**.

"Well, I suppose I could wait," the **troll** said with a sigh.

"I am alone and hungry. I will join my **brothers** in the **meadow** and get some nice and sweet grass to **eat**," said the **biggest billy goat gruff**.

"Who is that trippety tripping over my **bridge**?" roared the **troll**.

"Oh, it is only me. Please let me pass. I only want to go to the **meadow** to **eat** some sweet grass," said the **biggest billy goat gruff**.

"Oh no, you are not. I'm going to **eat** you," bellowed the **troll**.

"That's what you think!" shouted the **biggest billy goat gruff** angrily. He lowered his horns, galloped along the **bridge** and butted the ugly **troll**. Up, up, up went the **troll** into the air. Then down, down, down into the rushing river below. He disappeared below the swirling waters. "That taught him a lesson," said the **biggest billy goat gruff**. He continued across the **bridge** and met with his **brothers**, and they ate grass and played for the rest of summer.

Introduction: All the children sit in a circle. The teacher asks them what a troll looks like. Get the children to express their thoughts and ideas freely.

Role on the wall: Give an outline of an image and ask the children to write inside the image the different characteristics or personality traits of a troll. If they are too young to write, get them to draw inside the image.

Group work: Divide the class into smaller groups of 5 or 6 children. Each group works together to create the troll with their bodies.
Suggestions: One of them could be head, the others could be the bodies or the legs. They could be two heads, 10 legs, four hands, etc. Each group should be different.
Then ask each group to move around the room as the troll. The group should stay connected as they walk. Once they have mastered the movement they can make sound.

Still image: Get each group to make a still image of the troll. He should look as fierce and as scary as possible.

Teacher in role: The teacher assumes the role as the troll. She can do this by changing her voice or using a prop or putting on a costume. She sits on a seat which becomes the hot seat.

Hot-seating: Each child in the class asks the troll a question.
Suggestions: Why does the troll live by himself?
Where is his family?
Why does he not like the billy goats?
Does he not have any friends?
Why does he live under a bridge?

Voice production (pitch and power): Divide the class into groups of three. They each must assume the role of one of the

billy goats. They should experiment with the pitch and power of each of the billy goats.
The smallest goat should have a soft and high-pitched voice.
The middle size goat should have a medium volume and medium-pitched voice.
The biggest goat should have a loud and low-pitched voice.
Give each group time to find their voices.

Choral speaking: Get each group to practice saying the following together:

"Please, Mr Troll, may we cross the bridge so we can graze on the green grassy ridge?"

Get them to say it first as the smallest goat, then the middle sized goat and then finally the biggest goat.

Thought tracking: The teacher tells each group they are going to cross the bridge. She taps each goat on the shoulder, and they must say how they feel about crossing the bridge and confronting the goat. The teacher can extend this by asking each goat what they will say to the troll.

Conscience alley: The class forms two lines facing each other. The line on the left must think of reasons why the troll should eat the billy goats. The line on the right should think of reasons why the troll shouldn't eat the billy goats.

Teacher in Role: The teacher walks down the centre of the line as the troll and she listen to each reason carefully.

Improvisation: Divide the class into pairs. One child is the biggest billy goat and the other is the troll. They must come up with alternative ending. The goat doesn't throw the troll into the river. They can act out an alternative and most positive ending.

Closure: Both the troll and billy goats should have been mindful of each other's feelings. Invite the children to participate in the following mindfulness activities.

Heartbeat exercise: Ask the children to stand up and jump up and down, run on the spot or do jumping jacks for a minute. At the end of the minute, get the children place their hand on their hearts and pay attention to how their heartbeat and their breathing feels.

Breathing with a pinwheel: Give each child a pinwheel. Get them to blow on their pinwheels using long, deep breaths, and notice how they feel. Ask the following questions - Do you feel calm and relaxed? Is it easy or hard to sit still? Now blow on the pinwheels using short, quick breaths. How does your body feel now? Do you feel the same way after breathing quickly as you did after breathing slowly? Now blow on the pinwheels normally. How does this feel? What did you notice about how different ways of breathing makes you feel?

Other Books by the Author:

Drama Start Series:

Drama Start: Drama Activities, Plays and Monologues for Children (Ages 3-8)

Drama Start Two: Drama Activities for Children (Ages 9-12)

Stage Start: 20 Plays for Children (Ages 3-12)

Movement Start: Over 100 Movement Activities and Stories for Children

ESL Drama Start: Drama Activities and Plays for ESL Learners

On Stage Series:

Aesop's Fables on Stage: A Collection of Plays Based on Aesop's Fables

Fairytales on Stage: A Collection of Plays for Children

Classics on Stage: A Collection of Plays Based on Classic Children's Stories

Christmas Stories on Stage: A Collection of Plays for Children

Panchatantra on Stage: A Collection of Plays for Children

Hans Christian Andersen's Stories on Stage: A Collection of Plays for Children

Oscar Wilde's Stories on Stage: A Collection of Plays Based on Oscar Wilde's Short Stories

Just So Stories on Stage: A Collection of Plays Based on Rudyard Kipling's Just So Stories

Animal Stories on Stage: A Collection of Plays Based on Animal Stories

More Fairytales on Stage: A Collection of Plays Based on Fairytales

Irish Legends on Stage: A Collection of Plays Based on Irish Legends

Bible Stories on Stage: A Collection of Plays Based on Bible Stories

Buddha Stories on Stage: A Collection of Plays Based on Buddha Stories

Bird Stories on Stage: A Collection of Plays Based on Bird Stories

Grimm's Fairytales on Stage: A Collection of Plays Based on the Brothers Grimm's Fairytales.

www.ingramcontent.com/pod-product-compliance
Lightning Source LLC
Chambersburg PA
CBHW021158080526
44588CB00008B/397